Company Carswell

Carswell & Co.'s Catalogue of Second-Hand Law Books

Embracing portions of the libraries of the late Hon. Chief Justice

Wallbridge, Hon. Mr. Justice O'Connor, Hon. Judge Daniell, John Dewar,

Esq., the Hon. Mr. Justice Ramsay, D. Mitchell

Company Carswell

Carswell & Co.'s Catalogue of Second-Hand Law Books
*Embracing portions of the libraries of the late Hon. Chief Justice Wallbridge, Hon.
Mr. Justice O'Connor, Hon. Judge Daniell, John Dewar, Esq., the Hon. Mr. Justice
Ramsay, D. Mitchell*

ISBN/EAN: 9783337064631

Printed in Europe, USA, Canada, Australia, Japan

Cover: Foto ©Suzi / pixelio.de

More available books at **www.hansebooks.com**

CARSWELL & CO.'S

CATALOGUE OF

SECOND-HAND LAW BOOKS

EMBRACING

PORTIONS OF THE LIBRARIES

OF

THE LATE HON, CHIEF JUSTICE WALLBRIDGE, HON. MR. JUSTICE
O'CONNOR, HON. JUDGE DANIELL, JOHN DEWAR, Esq.,
THE HON, MR. JUSTICE RAMSAY, D. MITCHELL
McDONALD, Esq., AND OTHERS.

———

IN THIS CATALOGUE

THE PUBLISHERS OFFER SOME GOOD BARGAINS

——IN——

TEXT BOOKS AND REPORTS.

———

ADDRESS—

CARSWELL & COMPANY

LAW PUBLISHERS, ETC.

28 ADELAIDE STREET EAST. TORONTO, ONT.

LETTERS TO A LAW STUDENT

—BY—

JUNIUS JESSEL BURKE

—OF—

OSGOODE HALL, BARRISTER-AT-LAW.

THIS IS A BOOK OF SOME 80 PAGES,

—CONTAINING—

LETTERS OF INSTRUCTION TO

1st. The YOUNG MAN who thinks of Studying Law ; 2nd. To the one who has LAUNCHED FORTH ; on How to Read Law Books ; *Legal Definitions*, *Difficulties of Reading*, how to overcome. *Professional Success*—upon what it depends.

How to learn PRACTICE & PLEADING, ATTENDING COURT SITTINGS, HOW TO STUDY TRIAL PROCEDURE, RULES OF PROFESSIONAL CONDUCT, LAWYERS' MOTTO, Etc., Etc.

TO WHICH IS ADDED

AN APPENDIX OF EXAMINATION PAPERS

Giving an idea of the kind of Questions generally submitted to Students at Osgoode Hall.

Sent Post-paid on Receipt of Price, $1.00, in Cloth Binding.

ADDRESS

CARSWELL & CO.,

LAW PUBLISHERS, ETC.,

26 & 28 Adelaide St. E., Toronto

A Book of Humorous and Entertaining Anecdotes

BEARING ON

LAW, LAWYERS, WITNESSES, JURIES, OFFICERS
OF COURT, ETC., ETC.

As nothing is so well calculated to preserve the healthful
action of the human system as a good hearty
laugh; it is with this view this
collection has been
published.

SAMPLES:

"I do not say," remarked a lawyer, "that the defendant in this case is a thief; but I do say that if his farm joined mine I would not try to keep sheep."

"A Cincinnati lawyer recently won a $2,000,000 contested will case and turned over to the defendant over $500,000 of the amount. The other lawyers did not understand his generosity until they learned that he was engaged to marry his client's daughter, and expected to get the money back."

SPLINTERS make a Book of 279 pages, printed on good paper, Bound in Cloth, sent to any address, carriage prepaid, on receipt of
Price, $1.00.

A DIGEST

—OF—

ALL CASES DECIDED BY THE SUPREME COURT OF CANADA

Since it's Organization in 1875 to the 1st of May, 1886.

BY ROBERT CASSELS, Q.C.

REGISTRAR OF THE COURT.

———————————

THE DIGEST comprises a summary, not only of the Reported Cases, of which ten volumes have been completed, but also of the Unreported Cases. Of the Unreported Cases there are about two hundred, with Notes.

The DIGEST will be found a ready volume of reference to them, by merely adding the volume and page of the Report, at the end of each case, in the List of Cases in the DIGEST.

All cases bearing upon the Jurisdiction of the Supreme Court, about forty in number, will be found under that heading; and many cases on Insurance, Fire, Life and Marine, and the Liabilities and Powers of Railway Companies, not yet reported, will be found under appropriate titles, as well as all the constitutional cases decided by the Court.

The DIGEST will contain also many decisions (about 100) by the Court and the Judges on important Points of Practice, relating to time, security, case, fatcums, agents, counsel, settling and amending orders, etc.

Where a case has been reported in the Court below, reference has been made to the volume in which it will be found, and especial care has been taken with the Unreported Cases to state the facts and points fully.

———————————

HALF-CALF, $10. SENT CARRIAGE PREPAID ON RECEIPT OF PRICE.

———————————

Address

CARSWELL & CO.,

LAW PUBLISHERS, · *TORONTO, CANADA*

INDEX-DIGEST

OF

LAW REPORTS FOR 1887

Of Ontario, Nova Scotia, New Brunswick, Manitoba, Prince Edward Island, British Columbia, Selected Cases from Quebec and Supreme Court of Canada.

The Canadian Law Times.

E. DOUGLAS ARMOUR, Esq.,

(OF OSGOODE HALL.)

BARRISTER-AT-LAW, EDITOR.

E. B. BROWN, Esq.,

(OF OSGOODE HALL.)

BARRISTER-AT-LAW, EDITOR OF NOTES OF CASES.

To increase the general satisfaction with which the CANADIAN LAW TIMES has been received by the Profession since its first appearance, seven years ago, the Publishers have arranged with the Editor of the Notes of Cases that the Index-Digest to Vol. VII. of the CANADIAN LAW TIMES "Occasional Notes" shall be a Digest not only of the cases reported and noted in that volume, but also of all the cases reported during 1887 in the regular series of Reports of above named Courts. More than sixty of the cases—many of them of great importance—are not reported elsewhere than in the C. L. T. Where a case is to be found both in the TIMES and in a regular Report, the reference is to both.

It will also give a Summary of such cases as may only appear in the Official Reports, thus making an Index and Digest of the Reported and Decided Cases to the end of 1887 for the Dominion of Canada.

No extra charge to subscribers to the C. L. Times for 1888.

The CANADIAN LAW TIMES for 1888 will continue to give Notes of Cases in all the Courts of the various Provinces, Articles of General Interest, Reviews of Exchanges, Book Notices, etc., etc.

The Publishers have compiled an Almanac in form of a Blotting Pad, 18 x 24 inches, on which is printed Useful Information, such as Calendar, Table of Descent of Real and Personal Property of Intestates in Ontario, the Judiciary of Canada, County and Judicial Officers, etc., which will be PRESENTED TO EACH SUBSCRIBER to the CANADIAN LAW TIMES for 1888. Price of Pad alone, $1.00.

SUBSCRIPTION TO CANADIAN LAW TIMES, $5, PAYABLE IN ADVANCE.

The First Seven Volumes may be had Bound in Half-calf at the unbound Price, Namely, $35.

CARSWELL & CO.,

LAW PUBLISHERS, Etc.,

26 & 28 Adelaide St. East, - TORONTO, Ont

CARSWELL & CO.'S
CATALOGUE

OF

SECOND-HAND LAW BOOKS.

ABBREVIATIONS. Binding, state of, is indicated by the letters
"a,b,c." a, means good binding ; b, means cloth binding, or leather
in fair condition ; c, means binding is either paper or of no account.
"**Am.**" means published in the United States ; "**Can.**" published in
Canada, most of the other books are published in London.
Where a book is in two or more volumes, price given is for entire
work unless otherwise ordered.

TEXT BOOKS.

A

Abbott's Digest of Corporations. 1869. Am., *a* $5. *c* $4.
    b $4.50. 1879. *a* $6.
        on Shipping. 1812. *b* 25c. 1840. *c* 50. 1844.
            c 50*. Am., 1850. *b* $1. 1854. *b* $1.25.
        Insolvent Act. Can., 1864. *b* 25c.
Abdy & Walker's Gaius. 3 copies. 1876. *b* each $2.50.
Acts Relating to Justice of Peace. Can., 1853. *b* 25c.
Adams on Ejectment. 1812. *b* 25c. 1818. *b* 25c. 1840.
    Am. *a* 50c. 1846. *b* 50c. 1846. *c* 50c.
        on Equity. Am., 1855. *b* $1.50. 1859. 2 copies.
            b each $2. 1873. *a* $3.50.

Addison on Contracts.   1857.   Am., 3 copies.   *b* each $1.
    1869. 3 copies. *b* each $3. 1875. *a* $5. 1849.
    2 copies. *b* each 50c. 1862. *a* $1.50. Am.,
    2 vols. 1883. *a* $10. 1 vol. 1883. *a* $10.
   on Torts. 1864. *c* $2.50. 1869. *a* $2.50. 1870.
    2 copies. *a* each $3. 2 vols. 1876. Am.
    a $4. 1879. *a* $4. *c* $3.
Allison's Prac. Crim. Law.   Scot., 1833.   *b* $2.
Allen's Rules of Court.   Can., 1847.   *b* 25c.
   Telegraph Cases.   Am., 1873.   *a* $4.
American Railway Cases.   2 vols.   Am., 1854.   3 copies.
   b each $4.   1857.   *a* $4.
   Municipal Corporations.   Vol. ii.   1874.   *b* $2.
Amos & Ferard on Fixtures.   1827.   3 copies.   *b* each 50c.
   2 copies.   *c* each 25c.

Anderdon on Duties of Church-wardens.   1824.   *c* 50c.
Anderson's Digest Common and Crim. Law.   1867.   *b* 50c.
Andrew's and Stoney's Judicature Acts.   1880.   *b* $1.
Angell on Adverse Enjoyment.   1827.   Am.   *a* $1.
   on Carriers.   Am., 1849.   *a* 75c.   1849.   *c* 50c.
    1868.   *b* $2.
   and Ames on Corporations.   Am., 1832.   *b* 50c.
   on Highways.   1886.   *a* $5.50
   on Insurance.   Am., 1855.   2 copies.   Latest.   *b*
    each $3.
   on Limitations.   1876.   3 copies.   *a* each $5.50.
Anson on Contracts.   1879.   *c* $1.25.   1882.   2 copies.
   a each $2.   1882.   *c* $1.
Anthon's English and Latin Lexicon.   Am., 1849.   *a* 50c.
   1853.   *c* 50c.
Archbold on Awards.   1861.   *b* 75c.
Archbold's Bankruptcy Practice.   1844.   2 copies.   *b* each
   25c.
    Bankruptcy.   B Griffiths & Holmes.   1867.   2
     vols.   *a* $4.
    Crim. Pleadings.   1856.   2 copies.   *b* each $1.
     1875.   2 copies.   *a* each $4.   1878.   *a* $5.
    Jervis Acts.   1851.   *b* 25c.

Archbold's Modern Prac. 1834. *b* 50c.
      Parish Officer. 1855. *b* 50c.
      Peel's Acts. 2 vols. 1830. *b* 25c.
      Queen's Bench Practice. 1838. *b* $2. 1840.
        b $1.50. 2 vols. 2 copies. 1847. *a* each
        50c. 1855. 3 copies. *c* each $1.50.
        1856. *c* $2. 1858. 2 copies. *b* $3.
        1862. 4 copies. *b* each $7. 1866. 2 copies.
        Latest edition under C. L. P. Act. *a* each
        $10.
      Q. B. Division Practice. The 1885 edition is
        under new English Rules later than On-
        tario Rules. 2 vols. 1879. 3 copies.
        a each $10. 4 copies. *b* each $9.
Arnould on Marine Insurance. 2 vols. 1848. *a* $1.
      1872. *c* $5. 1877. 3 copies. *b* each $9.
Ashley on Attachment. 1819. *b* 50c.
Atherley on Marriage Settlements. 1813. 2 copies. *c*
      each 25c. 2 copies. *b* each 50c.
Atkinson's Theory and Practice of Conveyancing. 2 vols.
      1839. *c* $1.
      Real Property. 1833. *c* 25c.
Attorney's Pocket Book. 1734. *c* 25c. 1764. 2 copies.
      c each 25c.
Ayckbourn's Chancery Practice. 1855. *b* 25. 1858.
      b 50c. 1861. *c* 75c.

B

Babington on Set-Off. 1827. *b* 50c.
Bacon on Leases. 1798. *c* 50c.
Bailey's Bills of Exchange. 1799 and Tables 1807 in 1
      vol. *a* $1
Bainbridge on Mines and Minerals. 1849. *a* 50c.
Baker on Burials. 1855. *b* 25c.
Ball on Torts. 1880. *b* $3.50.

Banning on Limitations. 1877. *a* $3.50; *b* $3.

Barclay's U. S. Constitution. Am. 1878. *b* 25c.

Barnham's Series of Questions of Legal Education. 1840.
    b 50c.

Barry on Conveyancing. 1865. *a* $1. *b* 75c.

Barton's Conveyancer and Bird's Sup'lt. 1821. 7 vols.
        wtg. vol. 2. *c* $1.50. 5 vols. 1811. *b* $1.
    Forms of Conveyancing. Vol. 1. 1827. *h* 25c.

Batten on Contracts. Am., 1849. *a* $1.

Bayley on Bills. 1812. *h* 50c. *c* 25c.

    Blackstone. 1840. *c* 50c.

    on Fines, etc. 1828. *a* 50.

Beames' Costs, 1822. 3 copies. *a* 50c. 3 copies. *b* each 25c.

Beaumont on Bills of Sale. Am., 1855. 2 copies. *b* each
    50c. 1860. 2 copies. *a* each $1.

Beccaria on Crimes. Am., 1872. *b* 1.

Beck's Medical Jurisprudence. 1842. *a* $1.50. *c* $1.

Bedford's Final Examination Digest. Latest. 1879. *b* $2.
    Final Examination Guide to the Judicature Acts.
        1875. *b* $1.

Beebee's Anthon's Blackst . . Am., 1837. *b* 50c.

Bell's Excise Law. 1873. *b* ?.

Benjamin on Sales. Am., 18.,5. *a* $2.

    St. Alban's Raid. Can. 1865. 3 copies. *c*
    each $3.

Bennet's Biographical Sketch Book from Note Books of a
    Law Reporter. 1867. *b* $2.

    Fire Insurance Cases. 1729-1875. Am., 1872.
        5 vols. *b* $15.

    Master's Office. 1831. *b* 50c.

    Receivers. 1869. *a* $1.

Bentham. The Packing of Special Juries. 1821. *c* 50c.

Bentham's Theory of Legislation. 1876. *b* $1.

Best on Evidence. 2 vols. Am., 1876. 2 copies. each $3.
    1866. *a* $1. 1849. *b* 50c.

Best's Right to Begin and Reply. Am., 1880. *b* $1.
    1837. *b* 25c.

    on Presumption. Am., 1844. Scarce. *b* $2.

Bigelow on Estoppel. Am., 1876. 2 copies. *a* each $2.50.

Torts. Am., 1882. *b* $1.50.

Billing on Pews. 1845. *a* 50c.

Bingham on Infancy, etc. 1816. *b* 50c.

on Descents. Am., 1875. *a* $3.

Bird's Pocket Conveyancer. 2 vols. 1830. *c* 50c.

Bishop on Contracts. Am., 1878. 3 copies. *a* each $1.

on Married Women. 2 vols. Am., 1878-5. *a* $10.

Bispham Principles of Equity. Am., 1878. *a* $3.

Bissett on Partnership. 1847. *c* 50c. *b* 75c.

Blackstone's Commentaries. 4 vols. 1793. *c* $4.

Law Tracts. 2 vols. 1762. 2 copies. *c* $1 each. 1771. *c* $2.

Blackwell on Tax Titles. Am., 1855. 2 copies. *b* $1 each.

Blainey on Life Annuities. 1817. *c* 50c.

Blumenstiel on Bankruptcy. 1878. *a* $1.

Boscawen on Conviction. 1792. *b* 50c.

Boote's Action at Law. 1766. *b* 25c. 1823. *c.* 50c.

Botsford's Rules of Court. Can., 1865. *a* 25c.

Bowyer's Public Law. Am., 1854. *b* $1.

Two Readings on Jurisprudence & Roman Law. 1850. *b* 50c.

Boys on Coroners. Can., 1864. 2 copies. *a* each 50c. 1878. *a* $2.

Brady on Executors. 1845. *b* 50c.

Bradby on Distresses. 1808. *c* 25c.

Brice on Ultra Vires. 1874. *b* $2.50. 1877. 2 copies. Latest *a* each $8.50.

Bridgman's Digest of the Early Chan. Reports. 3 vols. 1805-24. *b* $2.

Bright on Husband and Wife. 2 vols. 1849. *b* $3. Am., 1850. *b* $3.

Brightly's Bankruptcy. Am., 1869. *b* 25c.

Broom's Common Law. 1864. *b* $1.50. Am., 1873. *b* $2.50.

Broom & Hadley's Commentaries on the Law of England. 4 vol. 1869. *c* $5. 2 vols. Am., 1875. *b* $6.

Legal Maxims. 1870. *a* $3.

Browne Savigny's Roman Law of Obligation. 1872. *a* $1.
    on Sales. 1821. *c* 50c.
    Medical Jurisprudence of Insanity. 1871. *b* $2.50.
    Civil and Admiralty Law. 2 vols. 1802. *b* $1.
    on Probate. 1873. *a* $1.
    and Chadwick's Examination Questions at Osgoode
            Hall. 1862. 2 copies. *a* each $1.50.
Brough on Elections. 1871. *a* $1.
Bryant & Stratton's Commercial Law. Am., 1861. *b* $1.
    1863. *b* $1.
Bullen & Leake's Precedents of Pleading. 1860. *b* $3.
    1868. 4 copies. *b* each $5. *c* $4.
Bullers Nisi Prius. 1790. *b* 50c. 1791. *c* 50c. 1817.
    2 copies. *b* each $1. *c* 50c.
Bunyon on Fire Insurance. 1867. 2 copies. *c* each $1
    on Life Insurance. 1868. *c* $1.50. 1868. *b* $1.50.
            Supplement, 1870. *c* 50c.
Barlamaqui's Natural and Political Law. Am., 1859.
    b $1.
Burrill on Assignments. 1877. *a* $2.50. 1882. *a* $3.50
    on Circumstantial Evidence. Am., 1856. *a* $1.
Burn's Ecclesiastical Law. 4 vols. 1747. *b* $1.50.
Burge on Suretyship. 1847. *c* 50c. 1849. *a* $1.
Burrough & Gresson Irish Equity Pleader. 1842. *b* 50c.
Burton on Real Property. 1830. *b* 50c. 1837. *c* 50c..
    Am., 1839. *b* 50c. 1845. *a* $1. *c* 50c. 1856.
    b $2.50.
Bushby on Elections. 1868. *b* 75c. 1874. *b* $1.
By-laws of Toronto, consolidated. 1870. *a* $2. 1876.
    a $5.
Byles on Bills. Am., 1856. *a* 75c.

C

Cabinet Lawyer. 1853. *b* 50c.
Caldwell on Arbitration. 1825. *a* 50c.
Calvert on Parties to Suits in Equity. 1837. *c* 25c.

Campbell's Lives of the Lord Chancellors. Complete set.
10 vols. 1856. *b* $6.

 on Negligence. 1871. 2 copies. *b* each $1.50
1878. *b* $2.50.

Cameron's Opinions. 1878. *a* $1.

 Digest. 1840. 2 copies. *b* each 50c. 1841.
b 75c.

 Rules of Court. Can., 1844. 2 copies. *b* each
50c. *c* 25c.

Canada Law Journal. Old series. 1855-64. 10 vols.
a $40.

Canada Law Journal. New series. 1865-87. 22 vols.
a $90.

Canadian Conveyancer. 1859. *b* 75c. 1879. *b* $1.

Canning's British Oratory. Vol. ii. Am., 1842. *b* 50c.

Capgraves Liber de illustribus Henricis. 1858. *b* $2.

Carter's Justice of the Peace. Can., 1856. *c* 50c.

Cassels Manual Supreme Court. Can. 1877. *b* $2. 1877-84.
a $3.

Cavanagh on Money Securities. 1879. 2 copies. *a* each $3.

Chalmers Bills of Exchange. 1878. *a* $1.50. 1881. 3
copies. *b* each $2.

 Colonial Opinions. Am., 1858. 3 copies.
a each $4.

Chambers & Peterson on Railways. 1848. *a* $1.

Chance on Powers. 2 vols. 1831. *c* $1.

Chancery Orders. Can. 1868. *a* 50c. 1876. *c* $5.

 Rolls. Lord Plunkett's Orders. 1834. *a* 50c.

Charley's Judicature Act. 1877. 2 copies. *c* each 50c.

 Real Property Statutes. 1874. *b* 50c.

Chitty on Bills. 1818. *c* 25c. 1833. 2 copies. *b* each
50c. 2 vols. 4 copies. 1834. *b* each $1.25.
c $1. 1839. Am., *b* 75c. 1840. *c* $1. Am.,
1842. 2 copies. *b* each $1. *c* 75c.

 Commercial Lawyer. 1853. *c* $1.

 Laws of Commerce. 4 vols. 1824. 1 and 2 *a*
scarce. 3 and 4 *c* $12.

Chitty on Contracts. 1841. *b* 25c. 1850. . *c* 25. 1853.
    c $1. Am., 1848. *b* 25c. 1844. *b* 25c.
    1866. *c* $1. 1874. 2 vols. *a* $6. 1876.
    a $7.

    on Descents. 1825. *b* 50c. *c* 25c.

  · Equity Index. 2 vols. 1831. *a* 50c. 4 vols. 1837.
    a $1. Am., 1853. 2 copies. *c* each $3.

    & Forster's Digest, C. L. Reports, Conveyancing
    and Bankruptcy. 1558 to 1840. 1841. *c* $3.

    Forms. 1840. *a* 50c. 1856. 3 copies. *b* each
    $1. *c* 2 copies each 75c. 1847. *c* 2 copies
    each 50c. 1847. *a* 75c. 1858. *c* $1. 1866.
    A latest under C. L. P. Act. *a* $5.

    on The Game Laws. 1826. *b* $1.

    on Pleading. 2 vols. 1809. *b* 25c. 3 vols. 1844.
    b $3. *c* $2. 1847. *a* $1.25. 2 vols. 1876.
    a latest Ed. $13.

    Practice. 3 vols. 1837. *b* $3. Am., 4 vols. 1836.
    b $2.

    Precedents of Pleading. Am., 1839. 2 vols. 2
    . copies. *b* each $1. 1847. *b* $1. 1847.
    a $1.25.

    Statutes. 4 vols. 1854. *c* $3.

Chronological Index. British Statutes. 1235-1886. *b* $1.
City of Glasgow Bank Trials. Paper. 10c. and 25c.
Clarke on Bills. Can., 1875. *a* $1.50.
    Criminal Law. Can., 1872. 3 copies. *a* each $2.
    1882. *a* $5.
    Insolvent Acts. Can., 1877. 3 copies. *a* each $1.
    Insurance. 1873-7. *a* $2.

Clement's Digest. Fire Insurance Decisions. 1872 to 1882.
    Am., *b* $3.

Cockburn's Ecclesiastical Courts, 1792. 2 copies. *a* 50c.
Code de Commerce, translated. 1826. *c* $1.
Coke's Abridgment. 1813. *b* 50c.
    First Institute. 1794. *c* $2. 2 vols. 1817.
    a $3. By Hargrave & Butler. 1832. *b* $8.

Cole on Ejectment. 1857. *a* Scarce.

Collectanæ Juridica. 2 vols. 1791. *b* $1.50.

Collyer on Partnership. 1832. 3 copies. *c* each 25.
Am., 1848. *b* 50c.

Colquhoun Judicature Acts. 1875. *b* $1.50.

Common Place Book Manuscript on various subjects.
b $1.

Comyns on Contract. 1824. *c* 25c.
Usury. 1817. *a* 25c.
Digest. 8 vols. 1822. *b* $8. *a* $10.

Conveyancing Precedents in Manuscript. 340 pp. *b* $1.

Cooke's Bankrupt Law. 2 vols. 1823. Latest, *a* $3.
on Defamation. Am., 1844. *a* $1. *b* 50c.
and Harwood's Charitable Trusts. 1867. *b* $2.

Cooley on Taxation. 1881. *a* $3.

Cooper's Equity Digest. 2 copies. 1868. *a* each $2. 3
copies. 1873. *a* each $1.
Equity Pleading. 1809. *b* 25c.
Justinian. 1841. *b* 50c.

Coote on Mortgage. 1821. *c* 25c. 1837. *a* 50c. Am.,
1850. 2 vols. *a* $1. 1884. *r* 50c.

Coote's Probate. 1878. *b* $5.

Copinger on Copyright. 1870. *a* $1.

Corner on Proceedings in Q. B. 1844. *a* $4.

Cornish on Deeds. 1828. *c* 50c. *a* 75c.
Remainders. 1827. *b* $1.
on Uses. Am., 1834. *a* $1.

County Courts Chronicle. 1847-49, 1861, 62, 63, 64, 65.
b each $1.

Couper's Trial of City of Glasgow Bank Directors. 1879.
b $4.

County Court Act of Manitoba. 1879. *b* 15c.

Coventry on Conveyancing. 1828. *c* 25c.
and Hughes' Digest. 2 vols. *b* $4.
Mortgage Precedents. 1826. *c* 50c.

Cox's Chancery Orders. 1861. 2 copies. *b* each 25c.
and Lloyd's County Courts. 1850. *b* 50c. *c* 25c.
Landlord and Tenant's Guide. 1853. *c* $1.

Crabb's History English Law. 1829. *a* $1.
    Conveyancing. 2 vols. 1845. *b* $2.
    Law of Real Property. 2 vols. 1846. 2 copies.
      a each $5. Am., 1846. *b* $5.
    Synonymes. 1824. *b* 50c.
Criminal Law. Considerations on. 1772. 2 copies.
      b each 25c.
    Statutes Canada. 1843. *b* 25c. 1867-81. *b* 50c.
Cribbs on Compensation. 1881. *b* $1.
    on the Church and Clergy. 1850. *c* 50c.
Crompton's K. B., etc., Practice. 1787. 2 vols. *b* $1.
Cross on Liens. Am., 1841. *a* $1.
Cruise on Fines. 1788. *b* 25c. 2 vols. 1794. *c* $1.
    on Uses. 1795. *c* 25c.
Crump's Marine Insurance. 1875. *a* $4.
Cunningham on Elections. 1877. *a* $1. 1880. 2 copies.
    a each $2.
Curtis' Equity Precedents. 1850. Am., *a* 25c. Am.,
    1859. *a* 25c.
    on Patents. Am., 1873. *a* $1.
Curson's Arcania Clericalia. 1705. *b* 25c.

D

Daniel's Chancery Practice. 1845. Am., 8 vols. *b* $2.
    3 vols. Am., 1851. *b* $2. 1865. *a* $5.
    2 vols. 1871. 9 copies. *b* each. $10.
    2 vols in 3. 1882 to 1884. Last edition.
    a $15.
    Forms. 1879. *a* $3.
Darby's Hand-book of Post Union Statutes. 1872. *b* $1.
Darling's Scintillae Juris. 1879. *b* 50c.
Dart on Vendors and Purchasers. 1876. Scarce, *c* $15.

Davidson's Banking Acts. Can., 1876. *b* $1.50
> Precedents of Conveyancing. 1873-81. 5 vols. in 8. *a* $25.
> Forms of Conveyancing. 1846. *b* 50c. *r* 25c.
> Concise Precedents. 1879. *a* $3.

Davis' Criminal Law Consolidation Statutes. 1861. *b* 25c.
> Registration. 1880. *b* $1.

Dawson's Attornies, etc. 1830. *r* 25c.

Dax Exchequer Practice. 1831. *c* 25c.

Davies' and Laurent's French Mercantile Law. 1855. *b* 50c.

Dawes' Epitome of Law of Landed Property. 1818. *b* 25c.

Deacon's Guide to Magistrates out of Sessions. 2 vols. 1843. *c* $1.

Debates on Confederation of Canada. 1860. *b* $2.

DeColyar on Guarantees. 1874. 2 copies. *b* each 50c. 1875. 2 copies. *a* each $1.

Dempsey's Magistrate's Hand-book. Can., 1860. *b* 25c.

Dickenson's Quarter Sessions. 1820. *b* 25c. 1841. *a* $1.

Digby on Transfer of Shares. 1868. *b* $1.
> History of the Law of Real Property. 1875. *b* $1.

Digest Modern Chy. Reports. 1807. *b* $1.

Dixon on Title Deeds. 2 vols. 1826. *c* 50c.

Doutre's Constitution of Canada. 1880. *a* $4.
> Procedure Civile de la Province de Quebec. 2 vols. 1867-9. *b* $3.50.

Draper on Dower. Can., 1863. 3 copies. *a* each $1.

Drewry Chy. Practice. 1856. *b* 75c.

Dubreuil's Reference Book or Index to Statutes of Canada. 1879. 2 copies. *a* each $1.50.

Duer on Marine Insurance. 2 vols. N. Y., 1845-6. *b* $10.

Du Ponceau on the U. S. Courts. 1824. *b* 25c.

Dutton's Justice of the Peace of Ireland. 1718. *c* 25c.

Dwarris on Statutes. 1830. 1 vol in 2 parts. *a* $2.

E

East's Pleas of the Crown. 1803. 2 vols. 2 copies. *c* each $4.

Eden on Injunctions. 1821. *a* 50c. *c* 25c. 1839. *b* $1.

Edgar's Insolvent Act. 1864. *a* 25c. 1869. *b* 50c. *c* 25c. 1875. 2 copies. *b* each $1.

Ellis on Insurance. 1832. *b* 25c. 1846. *a* $1.50.

Elme's Architectural Jurisprudence. 1827. *a* 50c. *b* 25c.

Elmer's Practice in Lunacy. 1844. *b* 25c. 1864. *c* 50c. 1877. *b* $3.

Elphinstone's Conveyancing. 1871. *b* $1.

Emden's Digest of Cases not in Law Reports. 1881. $1. 1882. 2 copies. *b* each $1.

    Complete Digest. 1883. *b* 2.75.

    Building Leases. 1882. *b* $5.

English C. L. R. Index. 2 vols. *a* $4.

Equity Pleader's Assistant. 1796. 2 vols. *b* 50c.

Euer's Pleading. 1791. 2 copies. *b* each. 25c.

Evans' Principal and Agent. 1878. *b* $6.

    Statutes. 1836. 10 vols. 2 copies. *b* each $5.

Everybody's Lawyer. Am., 1860. *b* 50c. Few pages short———

Every Man's Own Lawyer. 1864. *b* 75c.

Ewart's Index to Statutes. Can., 1874. *a* $1. 1878. *c* $1.

    Costs. Can., 1874. 5 copies. *b* each 50c. 1884. $1.

Ewell's Evans Agency. Am., 1879. *a* $4.

Exchequer Reports Digest. Am., 1855. 5 copies. *a* each $2.

F

Fearne's Contingent Remainders. 1791. *b* 50c. 2 vols.
      1844. Last edition. *a* $3.
      Posthumous Works. 1797. *c* 50c.
Fell on Mercantile Guarantees. 1820. *b* 50c.
Ferguson's Railway Companies. 1846. *c* 25c.
      Registration of Judgments. 1845. *b* 25c.
Field's Analysis of Blackstone. 1817. *c* 50c.
      Federal Courts. Am., 1883. *a* $3.
Finlason's Act. 1855. *a* 50c.
      Land Tenures. 1870. *a* $1.50.
      Leading Cases on Pleadings. 1847. *c* 50c.
Fisher's Common Law Digest. 5 vols. 1870. *a* $15.
      Supp., 2 vols. 1880. *a* $15. In all 7 vols.,
        fine copy. *a* $25.
      Annual Digests. 1878. *b* 50c. 1870-7. 9 years,
        and 1870-3 in 1 vol. *b* 50c. a year. 1876-
        78. *b* $4. 70-77. *a* $4.
      Criminal Law Digest. Am., 1871. $2.
      Mortgage. 1856. 2 vols. 2 copies. *b* $2. Am.,
        1857. Six copies. *a* each $1. 1868. 2
        vols. *b* $2.50. 1876. 2 copies. *a* $8.
Flander's Maritime Law. Am., 1852. *b* $1.50.
Flintoff's Real property. 1839. *b* $1.50.
Floyer's Proctor's Practice. 1746. *b* 50c.
Foard on Shipping. 1880. *a* $5.
Fonblanque on Equity. 2 vols. 1793-95. *a* 50c. 1820.
      c 75c. 2 vols. 1853. *b* $1.50.
Foran's Code of Civil Procedure of Quebec. 1879. 6
      copies. *a* each $2.
Form Book, by a Member of the Philadelphia Bar. 4
      copies. each 50c.
Forsyth on Trial by Jury. 1852. Scarce. *b* $3.

Fortesque's Delaudibus Legum Anglœa. Am., 1874. *b* $1.50.

Foster's Joint Ownership. 1878. *b* $1.50.

Foss' Judges of England. From 1066 to 1870. *b* $2.

Fowler's Exchequer Practice. 2 vols. 1817. *c* $2.

Fraser's Domestic Relations. 1846. 2 vols. *b* $2.

Freeman's Growth of the English Constitution. 1873. *a* $1.50.

Fremont's Index to Statutes. Can., 1884. *a* $1.50.

Fry's Specific Performance on Contracts. 1858. *b* 50c. 1871. *a* $1. 1881. *a* $5.

Fulbeck's Study of the Law. 1829. *c* $1.

G

Geldart's Hallifax on the Civil Law. 1836. *b* 50c.

Gerard on Titles to Real Estate. Am., 1869. *a* $1.

Gibbon's Contracts. 1875. *b* 25c.
　　　Roman Law, by Hugo of Gottingen. 1823. 4 copies. *c* each 25c.

Gibson's Law Examination Questions. 1880. *a* 50c.

Gifford's English Lawyer. 1827. *c* 25c.

Gilbert's Common Pleas. 1777. *c* 50c.
　　　Evidence. 1777. *c* $1. 1801. *c* $1.50.
　　　on Rents. Am., 1838. *a* 50c.
　　　on Tenures. 1824. *c* $1.
　　　on Uses and Trusts. 1811. *a* 50c.
　　　on Court of Exchequer. 1758. *a* $1.

Glen on Contracts, Engineers, etc. 1860. *a* 50c.

Goddard on Easements. 1877. *a* $2.50. 4 copies. *b* each $2.

Godefroi on Trusts. 1879. *c* $3. 1879. 3 copies. *a* each $3.50.

Goldsmith's Equity. 1853. *a* 50c.

Godson's Patents and Copyright. 1851. *c* $1.50.

Goodeve's Patent Cases and Suplt. 1876-8. 5 copies *b* each $2.

 Real Property. 1883. *b* $2.50.

Gowan's Rules of Court Canada. 1851. *b* 25c.

Gow on Partnership. 1823. *b* 25c. 1830. *c* 50c. 1841. *c* $2.

Grant on Banking. 1865. *b* $1. 1873. *a* $1.50.

 on Fixtures. 1845. *b* 25c.

 on Corporations. 1850. *b* $2.50. Am., 1854. *b* $2.50.

 on Trustees. 1830. *c* 50c.

Gray's Country Attorney's Practice. 1841. *c* 25c. 1854. *c.* 50c.

 on Costs. 1853. *c* $1.

G. W. Ry. Acts. Can., 1854. *b* $1.

Greaves and Lonsdale's Letter *re* Criminal Law. 1861. *c* 50c.

Greenwood on Conveyancing. 1882. *c* $1.50. 1865. *a* 50c.

 Real Property Statutes. 1878. 2 copies *b* each $1.

 and Martin's Magisterial and Police Guide. 1874. *b* $3.

Gresley's Equity Evidence. 1847. 2 copies *c* each 75 c. Am., 1848. *b* $1.

Griffith's Judicature Acts. 1875. 2 copies *a* each $1.

 Bankruptcy. 1869. *b* $2.

 Married Women's Property Act. 1875. *b* 25c.

 Institutes of Equity. 1868. 2 copies *b* each 1.

Gude's Crown Practice. 2 vols. 1828. *a* $2.

Gurdon's History of High Court of Parliament. 2 vols. 1731. *b* $1.

Gunning on Tolls. 1833. *a* 25c.

Gwynne on Probate, etc. 1836. *c* 25c.

H

Hallam and Delolmes' Constitutional History in 1 vol.
  1870. *b* 75c.

Hallilay's Examination Questions and Answers. 1859. *c*
  50c.

Hales' Common Law. Eng., 1820. Best edition. *c* $3.75.

Halsted's Law of Evidence. 2 vols. Am., 1856. *b* $1.

Hammond's Digest of Term Reports. 1819. 2 vols. *b*
  50c. 1824. 2 vols. *b* $1.

Hamilton on National Debt. 1813. *b* 50c.

Hancock's Index of Consol. Statutes of Can. and U. C.
           1865. 2 copies. *b* each $1.
        Conveyancing. 1861. *b* scarce $5.

Hand's Solicitors' Practice. 1808. *b* 25c.

Hanson's Probate Succession Duties. 1870. *b* 25c.

Hardcastle on Elections. 1874. *b* 25c.

Hardy's Legal Directory. 1883. *b* 50c.

Hare on Discovery. 1836. *c* 50c.

Harris' Criminal Law. 1884. *c* $2.50.
        Hint's on Advocacy. 1882. *b* 75c.

Harrison's Chancery Practice. 2 vols. 1791. *b* 50c.
           Digest (by Fisher). 4 vols. 1756-1843. 4 vols.
              c $2.50. 1756-1851. 7 vols. *b* $8.50.
           For year 1849. 1 vol. 1850. *b* 50c.
           Common Law Procedure Act. 1858. 8 copies.
              b 25c. 1870. Last edition. *b* $2. 2 copies
                a each $2.50. 5 copies *c* each $2.
           Municipal Manual. 1867. *c* 50c. 1878. *b*
              $5.
           & O'Brien's Digest. Can., 1863. 7 copies *b*
              each $2. 1868. *c* $1.50.
           County Court Rules, 1858, with Surrogate
              Court Rules. Can., 1864. *a* $1. *b* 75c.
. Hart's Mining Rights, etc. Can, 1867. *b* 25c.

Hatsell's Precedents of Proceedings in the House of Commons. 3 vols. 1786. *a* $2.

Hayes' Limitations to Heirs of the Body. 1824. *b* 50c.

Haynes' Chancery Practice. 1879. *b* $3.

      Equity. 1858. Am. 50c.

      Student's L. Cases. 1878. *a* $1.

Haywood's Ranks of the People. 1818. *c* scarce $3.

Hayward's Statutes on the Common Law Reports. 1832. *a* 50c.

Hayman's Joint Stock. Co.'s. 1874. *b* 50c.

Heard's Criminal Pleading. 1879. *a* $3.

Hennon's Louisiana Digest. 2 vols. 1861. Am., *b* $10.

Henley's Bankrupt Law. 1832. *b* 50c.

Heron's Jurisprudence. Am., 1873. *b* 75c.

Herman on Executions. Am., 1876. 3 copies. *b* each $2.

      on Estoppel. 1871. *b* $2.

Higgins on Watercourses. 1877. *a* $1.

Hill's Practice in Church Courts of Scotland. 1840. *b* $50c.

Hilliard's Sales of Personal Property. Am., 1869. *b* $2.

      Remedies for Torts. Am., 1867. *b* $2.

Hindmarch on Patents. 1846. 2 copies. *c* each $1, and *b* 75c. Am., 1847. 2 copies. *b* each $1.

Hind's Essay on Insects Injurious to Wheat. Can., 1857. *b* 50c.

Hodgin's Election Cases. 1883. *b* $5.

      Franchise Act. Can., 1886. *c* $1.50.

      Legal Directory. Can., 1879. *b* 25c.

      School Law Act. 1864. *a* 50c.

      Voters' List. Can., 1878. *c* $1.

Holdsworth's Wills. 1859. *c* 25c.

      Landlord and Tenant. 1861. *c* 25c.

      Practical Lawyer. 1878. 2 copies. *b* each $1.

Holland's Institutes of Justinian. 1873. *b* 75c.

Holland and Chandlar's Common Law Proc. Act. 1854. *b* 50c.

      Jurisprudence. 1872. *c* 75c. 2 copies. 1882. *b* each $2.

      Chancery. 1884. 2 copies. *a* each $3.

2

Holmsted's Judicature Practice. Can., 1881. 2 copies.
  b each $1.
Holroyd on Patents. 1830. *c* 75c.
Holt on Libels. 1816. *b* 25c.
Horrigan and Thompson's Cases in Self Defence. Am.,
    1874. *a* $5.
Houseman's Precedents of Conveyancing. 1861. *b* 50c.
Houston's Stoppage in Transitu. 1866. Last edition.
  b $2.25.
Hovenden on Fraud. 1825. *c* $2. Am. 2 vols. in 1.
    1832. *b* $2.
Howard's Colonial Law. 2 vols. 1827. 2 copies. *c*
    each $2.
      Duties of Solicitors of Real Prop. 1827. *c* $1.50.
      Excise and Customs. 1812. *a* $2.
      Rules and Practice of the Pleas and Equity sides
        of the Exchequer, in 2 vols. 1793. *b* $5.
Howell's Surrogate and Probate Practice. Can., 1880. 3
    copies. *a* each $5.
      Naturalization. 1884. *a* $1.50.
Hubback on Succession. 1844. *b* $1.
Hubbell's Legal Directory. 9th, 11th, 13th, 14th issues.
    1878-84. *a* each $1.
Hudson's Elective Franchise. 1832. *c* $1. *b* $1.50.
Hughes' Irish Chancery Prac. 1837. *c* 50c.
      Real Prop. 1849. 2 vols. *c* $1.50.
Humphrey on Real Property. 1827. 2 copies. *b* each 50c.
Hunt on Boundaries. 1870. 2 copies. *b* each 50c.
Hunter's Roman Law. 1876. *b* $5.
      Suit in Equity. 1860. Am., *b* 75c.

                    I

Ilbert's Judicature Practice. 1880. 6 copies. *b* each 25c.
Impey's Modern Pleader. 1814. *c* 25c.
      K. B. Practice. 1785. *b* 25c.

1881. 2 copies.

Defence. Am.,

1861. *b* 50c.
5. Last edition.

m. 2 vols. in 1.

7. 2 copies. *c*

). 1827. *c* $1.50.
$2.
and Equity sides
1793. *b* $5.
Can., 1880. 3

th, 14th issues.

1. *b* $1.50.
2.
.50.
ics. *b* each 50c.
each 50c.

5c.

es. *b* each 25c.

Indermaur's Leading Common Law Cases. 1873. *b* 50c.
    1874. 2 copies *b* 50c. 1875. *b* 75c.
    Leading Conveyancing and Equity Cases.
    1874. *b* 50c. 1881. 2 copies. *b* each $1.
    Manual of Practice. 1878. *b* $1.
Ingram on Compensation. 1864. 3 copies. *b* each 25c.
Innes' City of Glasgow Bank. 1878. *c* 25c.
    Digest of Easements. 1880. *h* 75c.
International Bridge Case. Am., 1881. *c* $1.

J

Jacob's Court Keeper. 1724. *b* 25c.
    Fisher's Digest to end of 1886. 11 vols. *a* $40.
    Law Dictionary. 6 vols. 1811. Am. *b* $2.
James' Bankrupt Law. Am., 1867. *b* 25c.
Jarman and Bythewood on Conveyancing. vols. 1 to 7, 9,
    11. 1841. *b* $5. Suplt to above. 1850.
    b 75c.
    on Wills. 2 vols. 1849. *h* $1. 2 vols. Am., 1859.
    b $1. 1861. *a* $3.
Jemmett's Equity. 1836. *c* 25c.
Jervis on Coroners. 1829. *a* 25c.
Jeremy's Digest of Common Law and Equity. 1825. *b* 75c.
Jenkin's New Clerk's Assistant. Am., 1857. *b* $1.50.
Jicklings' Estates and Alienations. 1829. 2 copies. *c*
    each 75c.
Johnson's Joint Stock Co.'s Bookkeeping. Can., 1881.
    b 50c.
Jones on Bailments. 1823. *b* 25c. 1833. 2 copies *c*
    each 50c. Am., 1836. *b* 75c. 1829. *c* 50c.
    1833. 2 copies. *a* each 75c.
    Constable's Manual. Can., 1882. *a* 50c.
    Prescription. Can., 1878. 4 copies. *a* each $3.

Joyce on Injunctions. 1872. 2 vols. *a* $10.
Junkin on the Oath. Am., 1845. *b* 50c.
Judicial Authority of the Roads. 1728. *c* 25c.

K

Kaufmann's Mackeldy's Roman Law. 1845. 3 copies.
    Vol. 1. *b* each $1.
Katchnevosky's Prize Law. 1867. *b* $1.
Keatinge on Family Settlements. 1810. *c* 25c.
Keele's Provincial Justice. 1858. *b* 50c. 1855.· *b* 25c.
    1864. *a* 50c. 2 copies. 1858. *c* each 25c.
Kekewich's Digest of Early Chan. Reports. 1804. *b* $1.25.
    2 copies. 1804. *c* each $1.
Kehoe's Choses in Action. Can., 1881. *a* $1.50.
Kennedy's Chy. Prac. 1852. 2 vols. *b* 50c.
Kent's Commentaries. 1 vol. Am., 1840. *b* $3.50.
            4 vols. Am., 1854. *b* $5.
    Commercial Law. 1837. *b* 50c.
Kerr's Action at Law. Am., 1854. 2 copies. *q* each 50c.
    Fraud and Mistake. 1883. Last edition. *a* $7.
    Magistrates' Act. Can., 1871. *b* $2.
    Common Law Procedure Act. 1852. 4 copies.
        b each 50c. 1854. *a* 75c.
    on Injunctions. 1878. *a* $6. Am., 1871. *b* $1.50.
Keyser's Law of the Stock Exchange. 1850. *a* 75c.
Kinne's Legal Directory. Am., 1854. *b* 25c.
Kirchner's Fugitive Offenders. 1882. *c* 50c.
Kirtland on Surrogate Courts of N. Y. Am., 1835. *b* 50c.
Kyd on Awards. 1791. *b* 50c.
    on Bills of Exchange. 1795. *b* 50c.

L

Laperrieres' Speakers' Decisions, H. of C. Canada. 1841-72.
18 copies. *b* each $1.
Lauderdale's Depreciation of the Paper Currency Proved.
1812-13. *a* $1.
Law Journal Digest.   1850-60.   2 vols. *a* each $2.
1850-65. *a* $2.   1 vol.   1850-65.   2 vols.
b each $1.75.   1855-65.   2 vols. *b* each
$2.50.   1860-65.   *b* $2 50.   1870-75.
a $2.50.   1870-75. *b* $2.50.   1870-75.
c $2.   1881-83. $2.50.
by Morgan and Williams.   vol. 1.   1803.
c scarce, $3.
Magazine.   Vol. 38 O. S.   1847. *a* $1.
Reports Digest.   1866-71. *b* $1. *c* $1.   2 vols. *a* $1.
1866-75.   2 vols. *a* $2. *b* $2.   1866-78. *a* $2.50.
b $2.50.   1865-85.   3 vols. *a* $17.
of Forfeiture for High Treason.   1798. *b* $1.50.
and Glanville's Parlt. Cases.   1761. *b* $1.   1793. *b* $2.
List (Eng.)   1858, '61, '70.   3 vols. *b* each $1.
Law's Patent and Copyright Laws.   1790-1870.   Am., 2
copies. *b* each $1.
Lawes' Charter Parties.   1813.   3 copies. *b* each $1.
on Pleading in Assumpsit.   1810. *b* $1.
Leake on Contracts.   1867.   3 copies. *b* each $2.   1878.
Last edition. *a* $9.
Lee's Bankruptcy.   1871. *b* $1.
Dictionary of Practice in Civil Actions.   2 vols.   1825.
c $1.
Shipping and Insurance.   1865. *b* 25c.
Lefroy and Cassels' Notes of Practice Cases under Jud.
Act Can.   1883.   2 copies. *b* each $1.
Leeming and Cross' Quarter Sessions.   1858. *b* $1.

Legal Examiner. 2 vols. 1832. *b* $2.

 Judicature in Chancery Stated (Lord King). 1727. *b* 50c. 2 copies. *a* each $1. 1828. *c* $1.

Leggo's Chancery Practice. 2 vols. 1876. Can. 3 copies. *b* each $10.

 Chancery Forms. Can., 1872. 2 copies. *b* each $1.50. 1876. *a* $3.

Leigh and Le Marchant on Elections. 1870. *b* 25c. 1874. 2 copies. *c* each 25c. *b* 50c.

Leith's Real Property Statutes. Can., 1869. 5 copies. *b* each $3.

 Blackstone Commentaries. 1864. 5 copies. *b* each $2.25. 1880. *b* $5.50.

Lely and Foulkes Judicature Acts. 1877. 6 copies. *a* each 50c.

Lewin on Trusts. 1837. *b* 25c. 1842. *b* 50c. Am., 1857. *c* $1. 1858. *b* 75c. 1879. 2 copies. *b* each $2.

Lewis on Conveyancing. 1863. *b* $1.

 on Equity Drafting. 1865. *c* $1.50. 1865. 6 copies. *b* each $2. 1865. 2 copies. *a* each $2.50. Index of the Ontario Statutes. 1884. 6 copies. *a* each $1.50. *b* $1.

 on Perpetuities. 1843. *a* $1.50

Lindley on Partnership. 2 vols. in 1. 5 copies. Am., 1860. *b* each $1. 1873. 2 vols. 2 copies. *b* each $6.

Littleton and B's Digest of Fire Insurance Cases. Am., 1868. *a* $1.50.

Liquor License Act of Ont. 1878. *a* 50c. 1884. *a* 75c. Compilation of. 1878-81. 75c.

Lloyd on Compensation. 1867. *b* 50c. 1870. *b* 75c.

Locke on Attachment. 1853. *b* $1.50.

Lorimer's Institution of Law. 1872. 2 copies. *b* each $3.

Lovelass on Intestacy. 1823. *c* 50c. 1823. 2 copies. *b* each 75c.

Lowry's Exchequer Equity Rules in Ireland. 1838. 2
   copies. *c* each 25c.
Lubes Equity Pleadings. 1840. *b* $1.
Ludlow's Joint Stock Cos. 1849. *c* 25c. 1850. *c* 25c.
Lund's Letters Patent. 1851. *a* 50c.
Lusignan's L. C. Reports Digest. 1872. *b* $1.
Lyon's Encumbered Estates. 1849. *b* 25c.
Lyon & Redman's Bills of Sale. 1877. *b* $1.

THE LAW LIBRARY.

The Law Library. Edited by Thos. Sargent, and J. C.
Lowber, of the Philadelphia Bar: 1838-1861. The
Law Library consists of some two hundred or more
elementary works of law, most of which are recog-
nized standard text books on their several subjects,
and though now old in date is still desirable, and
many of the volumes have never since been reprinted.
The Law library was published in seven series. We
have in stock the following, at prices mentioned. The
price refers to either 3rd, 4th, 5th, or 6th series. Exam-
ple 32 of 3rd series embraces 3 vols, as does Vol. 17 of
4th series, and Vol. 11 of 5th series, either of which is
$1.25.

THE LAW LIBRARY.	3rd Series.	4th Series.	5th Series.	6th Series.	
Bagley's Practice. Sugden on Powers, vol. 1.	5				1 00
Sugden on Powers, vol. 2. Byles on Bills.	6				75
Coote on Mortgages. Ward on Legacies.	8				1 00
Smith's Leading Cases, vol. 1. Babington on Auctions.	9				75
Atkinson on Titles. Watkins on Conveyancing. Gilbert on Rents.	10				1 25

THE LAW LIBRARY.	3rd Series.	4th Series.	5th Series.	6th Series.	
Powell on Devises, vol. 1 and part of vol. 2.	15				1 25
Loveless on Wills.					
Stock on Non Compo mentis					
Paley's Principal and Agent.					
Wilcock on Constable.		3			1 75
Worthington on Juries.					
Roscoe's Real Actions.	19	4			1 50
Shephard's Touchstone, vol. 1.		5			1 00
" " vol. 2.		6			1 00
Roper on Hus. and Wife, 2 vols.		7	1		1 00
Shelford on Marriage and Divorce.		8	2		1 50
Cross on Lien.	24	9	3		1 00
Eden on Bankruptcy.		10			1 00
Drewery on Injunctions.		11	5		1 25
Shelford on Mortmain, pt. 1.					
Shelford on Mortmain, pt. 2.			6		75
Woodesson's Lectures, vols. 1 and 2.		13	7		1 25
Woodesson's Lectures, vol. 3.					
Goldsmith's Equity Practice.	29	14	8		1 50
Pitman's Prin. and Surety.					
Wordsworth on Joint Stock Companies.	30	15	9		2 25
Joy on Confessions.					
Macpherson on Infants.					
Wills on Circumstantial Evidence.		16			2 25
Disset's Estates for Life.					
Preston on Merger.	32	17	11		1 25
Winslow on Insanity.					
Smith's Leading Cases, vol. 1.		18			50
" " vol. 2.		19	13		50
Brown's Action at Law.		20	14		1 00
Joy on Accomplices.					
Sewell on Sheriff.		21	15		1 00
Best on Presumptions (scarce)					
Miller on Equit. Mortgages.	37	22	16		3 50
Russell on Factors.					
Hubback on Succession to Real and Personal Property. (scarce).	38	23			1 50

Price	THE LAW LIBRARY.	3rd Series	4th Series	5th Series	6th Series
	Archbold's Nisi Prius, vol. 1.	39	24	18	50
1 25	" " vol. 2.				
	Broom's Legal Maxims.	40	25	19	2 00
	Bell's Contract of Sale.				
1 75	Tamlyn on Evidence.				
	Billing on Awards.	41	26	20	1 25
	Grady on Fixtures.				
1 50	Lewis on Perpetuities.	42	27	21	1 25
1 00	Notes to Recent Ld'g Cases.				
1 00	Archbold's Landlord and				
1 00	Tenant.	43	28		1 00
	Cooke on Defamation.				
1 50	Crabb on Real Property, vol.				
1 00	1 (scarce).	44	29	23	2 50
1 00	Crabb on Real Property, vol.				
1 25	2 (scarce).			24	2 50
	Smith on Contracts.				
75	Broom's Actions.	46	31	25	1 50
	Cole on Crim'l Informations.				
. 25	Pulling on Accounts.				
	Blackburn on Sale.		32		1 50
50	Phillimore on Domicil.				
	Lee on Abstracts of Title.		33		1 25
	Oliphant on Horses.				
25	Watson on Arbitration.		34		50
	Smith's Action at Law.				
	Worthington on Wills.				
25	Long's Discourses.			29	2 00
	Coode on Legislative Expressions.				
25	Byles on Bills.	51	36	30	1 25
	Williams on Personal Prop.				
50	Whiteworth's Eq. Precedents.	52	37		1 50
50	Notes of recent Ldg. Cases.				
00	Russell on Awards.		38		50
00	Sugden on Property.	54	39		75
	White and Tudor's L. C. in Equity, vol. 1.		40		1 00
50	Macqueen's Husband and Wife, pt. 2.				
	Supplement to Lewis on Perpetuities (scarce).		41		3 25
50	Best on Evidence.				

THE LAW LIBRARY.	3rd Series.	4th Series.	5th Series.	6th Series.	
Batten on Contracts. } Bell's Husband and Wife. }		42	36		2 00
Adams' Equity. } Forsyth's Infants. } Wildman's International Law, vol. 1. }	58	43			3 50
Coote on Mortgage.		44			1 00
Wildman on International Law, vol. 2.		45			1 00
White and Tudor's Leading Cases in Equity, vol. 2, pt. 1.	61				1 00
Foster on Scire Facias. } Lund on Patents. } Hindmarch on Patents. }	63				3 00
Wharton's Conveyancing. } Macnaghton's Select Cases. }		49		1	2 50
Smith's Master and Servant. } Kelly on Usury. }		50		2	1 00
Tapping on Mandamus (scarce).		51	45	3	4 00
Norman on Patents. } Collier on Mines. } Moore on Abstracts of Titles. } Pollock on Production of Documents. }		52		4	3 75
Woolrych on Waters. } Polson's Law of Nations. } Horne on Diplomacy. }		53		5	1 75
Bunyon on Life Insurance. } Locke on Attachment. } Sup. to Drewery's Injunctions }		54		6	2 50
Grant on Corporations.		55		7	2 50
Kerr's Actions at Law. } Dearsley's Criminal Process. }		56		8	1 00
Ross on Bills and Notes.		57		9	1 00
Phillimore's International Law, vol. 1. } Pothier on Partnership. }		58		10	2 25
Bowyer's Universal Public Law. } Levis Mercantile Law. }		59		11	1 50
Ross on Contract of Sale.		60		12	1 00

THE LAW LIBRARY.	3rd Series.	4th Series.	5th Series.	6th Series.	
Lindley's Study of Jurispru- dence (scarce).		61		13	2 50
Parsons on Wills.					
Coryton on Patents.	77	62		14	1 50
Macnamara on Nullities.					
Phillimore's International Law, vol. 2.		63		15	1 25
Smith's Real and Personal Property.				16	75
Cornish on Purchase Deeds.					
Jones' History of French Bar.		65		17	2 00
Broom's Common Law.	82	66			1 00
Mayne on Damages.					
Bucknell on Criminal Lu- nacy.		67			1 00
Grant on Banking.		68		20	75
Fisher on Mortgage.		69		21	2 25
Grapel on Roman Law.					
Phillimore's International Law, vol. 3.		7^			1 25
Robert's Principles of Chan- cery.		71		23	1 25
Powell on Evidence.					
Lewin on Trusts.				24	1 00
Haynes' Outlines of Equity.				25	50
Ross on Suretyship, Agency, Partnership & Insurance.		74		26	1 00
Fry's Specific Performance of Contract.				27	2 00
Phear on Waters.					
Westlake's Principles of In- ternational Law.		76		28	2 50
Appleton on Evidence.					
Lindley on Partnership, vol. 1.		77		29	75
Lindley on Partnership, vol. 2.		78		30	1 75
Beaumont on Bills of Sale.					
Trower on Debtor and Creditor.		79		31	1 75
Hunter's Suit in Equity.					

M

McArthur on Courts Martial, Naval and Military.   Vol I.
  1809.   *b* 75c.

McCall's Clerk's Assistant.   Am., 1875.   *b* $1.

McCord's Civil Code L. C.   1867.   *b* $1.   1870.   3 copies.
  b each $1.25.

McDougall's Law Lectures.   Can., Nos. 1, 2 & 3 in 2
  pts.   1882.   *c* each 50c.

McFarland's Equity Pleading.   1848.   *a* 25c.

McGibbon's Great Pew Case.   Can., 1877.   *b* $1.

Mackenzie's Dispositions in defraud of Creditors.   1675.
        c 75c.

          Institutes of the Law of Scotland.   1688.
              c 50.   1730.   *b* 75c.

Maclennan's Judicature Act.   1881.   7 copies.   *b* each
  $1.50.   1881.   *c* $1.   1884.   2 copies.   *a* each $4.

McMahon's Insolvent Act.   1875.   *a* 75c.   1875.   2 copies.
  c each 50c.

MacMillan on Costs.   Can., 1865.   2 copies.   *b* each 50c.

McNab Mag. Manl.   1865.   *b* 50c.

MacNamara on Nullities.   1842.   *a* 50c.   1842.   3 copies.
  c each 50c.

Macouns Manitoba and Great North West.   Can., 1882.
  b $1.

Macpherson on Infants.   1842.   *b* $2.

Macqueen's Husband and Wife.   1872.   *a* $2.   1840.
        a 50c.

          Divorce.   1858.   *b* 50c.

Maddock's Chy. Practice.   2 vols.   1815.   *b* 25c.   1837.
  c $1.   1837.   *b* $1.

Male on Elections.   1820.   *c* 50c.

Mallory's Entries.   2 vols.   1791.   *b* 75.

Manning's Exchequer Practice (C. P.).   2 vols.   1819.
  b $2.

Mansel on Limitations. 1889. *c* 25c.

on Demurrer. 1828. *b* 50c.

Marcey's Conveyancing Statutes. 1881. 3 copies. *b* each $1.

Maritime Court Rules. Ont., $1.

Markby's Elements of Law. 1871. *b* $1. 1874. *b* $1. 1875. *b* $1.25.

Marsden's Collisions. 1880. 2 copies. *b* each $2. 1880. *a* $2.

Marshall on Insurance. 2 vols. 1808. *b* 50c. 2 copies *c* each 50c.

Martin's Conveyancing. 1844. 5 vols. *b* $3.50.

Massachusetts Public Stats. 1882. *b* $3.

Matthews on Presumption, etc. 1827. *c* 50c.

on Portions for Children. 1829. *c* 50c.

Maxwell on Statutes. 1875. 3 copies. *b* each $2.50. 1879.

May's Parliamentary Practice. 1879. *b* $5. *a* $6.

Criminal Law. Am., 1881. Last edition. *a* $2.

Constitutional History. 1862. Vol. 2. Am. *c* 50c.

Mayne on Damages. 1856. *b* 50c. 1877. 5 copies *b* each $2.50. *a* $3.50. 1856. Am. *b* 50c.

Merrifield's Attornies and the Law of Costs. 1830. *c* 50c.

Michigan Compiled Laws. Vol. 2. 1872. *b* 50c.

Reports. Vol. 17 (Jennison 4). 1869. *c* $3.

Middleton Settled Estates Acts. 1878. *b* $1.

Miller on Land Tax. 1849. *a* 50c.

Mills on Eminent Domain. Am., 1879. 2 copies. *a* each $3.

Mitford's Chancery Pleadings. 1827. 2 copies. *c* each 50c. Am., 1840. *b* 50c. 1847. Last ed. 4 copies. *a* each $2.

By Tyler. Chancery Pleadings. Am., 1876. 2 copies. *b* each $2.

Moak's Argument in the Lowenstein Murder Case, Albany. 1874. Am., *a* $1.25.

Molesworth, Registration of Deeds. 1898. *b* 50c.

Molloy on Affairs, Maritime and Commerce. 1701. *b* 50c.

Montague's Opinions, by different authors, on The Punishment of Death. 1816. *c* $1. 1 copy. *a* $1.50.

Montague on Composition. 1823. *c* 50c.
    on Lien. 1821. *a* 50c. Am., 1824. *b* 50c.
    on Partnership. 2 vols. 1815. *c* $1.50.
    on Set-off. Am., 1825. *b* 50c.

Moore's Digest of Term Reports. Vol. 1. 1816. *c* 25c.
    Forms of Agreement. 1884. 2 copies. *a* each $3.

Morawetz on Private Corporations. 1882. 6 copies. *a* each $3.50.

More, Abridgment of his Reports by Wm Hughes. 1665. *c* $2. A curiosity.

Morgan's Attorneys Vade Mecum. 3 vols. 1792. *b* $1.
    Essays. 3 vols. 1789. *b* $1.
    Canadian Legal Directory. 1878. *b* 50c.
    Dominion, Annual Register. 1884-5. 2 vols. *c* 50c. 1880, 1881 & 1882. 2 vols. *b* each 25c.
    Chancery Acts and Orders. 1860. *c* 25c. 1862. 2 copies. *a* each $2. 1865. 2 copies. *b* each $2.50. 1862. *c* $1.50. 1882. *b* $5.

Morris and Finlason C. L. Procedure Act. 1852. *b* 25c.

Morse on Banking. Am., 1879. *a* $5.

Mozley and Whiteley's Law Dictionary. 1876. 2 copies. *a* each $3.50. 1876. *b* $3.

Municipal Act. 1866. Table and Index. Can. *b* 75c.

N

Napier's Practice Civil Bill Reports. 1843. *b* 50c.
Naval Trade and Commerce. 1788. *b* $2.50.
New Hampshire Laws. 1873. *b* $1.50.
New York Code. 1871. *a* 50c.
New York Legal Observer. 1843. Vols. 1, 2, 3, 5 & 6. *b* each 50c.

O

O'Brien's Division Courts Act. Can., 1866. *b* 75c. 1789.
    4 copies. *b* each $2. 1879-1885 in 1 vol. *a* $4.50.
Oke's Turnpike Laws. 1861. *b* 50c.
Oliver's Legal Tracts. 1833. *b* 50c.
Origin of Laws. Vols. 2 and 3. 1775. *a* 50c.
Orme's Digest of Election Laws. 1812. *c* 50c.
Osborne's Actions and Pleadings. 1844. *c* 25c.
Osgoodby's Directory. Am., 1881-2. *a* 25c.
O'Sullivan's Manual of Government. Can., 1879. 5 copies.
    b each 75c.
Outlines of Practical Law (by Editors of Law Chronicle).
    Law student's first book. 1858. *c* 75c.
Owen's Education Acts Manual. 1875. *b* 35c.

P

Palgrave's House of Commons 1869. *c* 50c.
Paley's Principal and Agent. 1819. *c* 50. 1819. *b* 25c.
            1833. 3 copies. *c* each 75c. Am., 1847.
            b 75c.
     on Convictions. 1838. *b* 50c.
Palmer's Company Precedents. 1867. *c* $4.
        Practice of the House of Lords. 1830. *b* 50c.
        1830. *c* 25c.
Paris and F.'s Medical Jurisprudence. 3 vols. 1823. *c* $1.
Park on Insurance. 2 vols. 1817. *b* $1.
    K. B. & C. P. Practice. 1829. *b* 50c.
Parker's Poor Laws. 1849. *c* $1.
Parkinson's Judge's Chambers. 1861. *c* 50c.
Parsons on Shipping and Admiralty. 2 vols. 1869. Last
    edition. 2 vols. *b* $10.
       Marine Insurance. 2 vols. Am., 1868. Last Edition.
       b $10.
     on Wills. Am., 1855. *b* $1.

Paterson, Fishery Laws of United Kingdom. 1863. *b* $1.
Patents of Canada. 1 vol. 1824-49, Pub. 1860. *a* $1.50.
Patrick's Election Cases. Can., 1851. *b* $3.
Peacock's Rules and Order of C. P. 1811. *b* 25c.
Peake's Law of Evidence. 1804. *b* 25c. 1813. *c* 25c.
    1813. *b* 25c.
Pearce's Guide to the Inns of Court. 1855. *b* 50c.
Pearson's Common Law Procedure Act. 1854. *c* 25c.
Peel's Acts. 1830. *c* 50c.
        Chancery Actions. 1878. *a* 50c. 1881. 2 copies.
        b each 75c.
Pemberton on Judgments. 1876. 4 copies. *b* each $2.
Penal Law, Principles of. 1771. 2 copies. *b* each 50c.
Perry on Trusts. 2 vols. Am., 1874. *a* $5.
Petgrave's Principal and Agent. 1887. *b* 75c.
Phear on Rights of Water. 1859. scarce. *b* $2.
Phillimore on International Law. 3 vols· 1854. Fine
    copy. *a* $4.
Phillips on Evidence. 2 vols. Am., 1840. *b* $1. 1851.
            4 vols. *b* $3.00. 1852. *c* $2. 1852. *b* $3.
            1854. *b* $2.50. 1867. *b* $4.
    on Lunatics. 1858. *b* $1.
Piggot's Conveyancer. 1739. *c* 25c. 1752. *b* 25c.
        on Foreign Judgments. 2 vols. Effect of, in
            English courts. 3 copies. 1879. *b* each $4.50.
        on effect of English judgment in foreign courts.
            1881. *b* $4.50.
        Recoveries. 1753. *b* 25c.
Pitt-Lewis' County Court Practice. 2 vols. 1883. *a* $5.
Platt on Leases, with Forms, etc. 1847. 2 vols. *b* $4.
        on Covenants. 1829. *c* $1.
Political Code, State of New York. Am., 1859. *c* 50c.
Pocock's Rules and Orders of K. B. 1811. *b* 50c.
Pollock's County Court Practice. 1857. 2 copies. *c* each
            50c. No title. *a* 75c.
        on Partnership. 1877. 2 copies. *b* each $1.
            1880. *b* $1. 1884. 3 copies. *b* each $1.50.
            Am., 1878. 2 copies. *b* each 50c.
        on Contracts. 1876. *a* $3. 1878. *a* $4.

Pomeroy's Constitutional Law. Am., 1875. *b* $1.50.
1885. *b* $4.

Pothier on Contract of Sale. Am., 1839. *b* $2.
on Obligations. 2 vols. Am., 1853. Scarce. 2
copies. *a* each $10.
on Partnership. 1854. *a* $1. Am., 1854. *b* $1.

Potter's Dwarris on Statutes. Am., 1871. 3 copies.
Last edition. *b* each $5.

Powell on Contracts. 1796. *c* $2.
on Evidence. Am., 1858. *b* 50c. 1859. *b* 75c.
on Mortgages. 1826. 2 vols. *c* $1.50.

Poynter's Practice in Ecclesiastical Courts. 1824. *b* 75c.

Prater on Husband and Wife. 1836. *b* 50c.

Pratt's Digest, Continuation of Jeremy's. 1855. *c* 25c.

Preston on Conveyancing. 1 vol. 1806. *c* 75c.
on Estates. 1820. *c* $1.50.
on Legacies. 1824. *b* 50c.

Prentice, Proceedings in an Action. 1877 *b* $1.50.

Price's Reversionary Payments. 1772. *b* 25c.

Priestly, Remarks on Blackstone. Vol. 4, as concerns
Dissenters. Am., 1773. *b* $1.

Principles of Common Law. 1858. *b* 50c.

Prior on Conveyancing. 1857. *a* $1.

Pritchard's Admiralty Digest, 1847. *c* $1. 1865. 2 vols.
2 copies. *a* each $6.

Protests, collection of. 1737. *b* $1.

Pulling on Attorneys. 1862. Latest. *b* $2.50. 1862.
a $3.
on Accounts. Am., 1847. *a* $1.00.

Public General Statutes. 30 & 40 Vic. 1876. *b* $1.

Q

Questions with Answers on Real Property and Conveyancing. 1839. *c* 50c.

3

R

Railroad Laws and Charters of the U. S.   By Gregg and
             Pond.   2 vols.   Am., 1851.   *b* $2.
Ram's Judgments.   Am., 1871.   *a* $2.50.
Ramshay's Rules of Pleading.   1838.   *c* 50c.
Rawle on Covenants for Title.   Am., 1854.   *b* $1.   1854.
             2 copies, each 50c.
Rawliuson's Municipal Corporation Act.   1850.   *b* 25c.
             1868.   *b* $1.50.
Reddie's Maritime Laws.   1841.   2 copies.   *h* each $1.
             Roman Law.   1826.   *c* $1.
             Science of Law.   1840.   2 copies.   *b* each $1.
                  1847.   2 copies.   *c* each $1.50.
             International Law.   1851.   *b* $1.50.
Redfield and B.'s Cases on Bills of Exchange and Notes.
             1871.   *b* $3.

             on Railways.   Am., 1859.   2 copies.   *b* each $1.50.
Reed's American Law Studies.   1882.   Last edition. $4.50.
Reeve's History of English Law.   1787.   4 vols.   *b* $2.
Repp's Trial by Jury.   1832.   *c* $1.50.
Revised Statutes N. Y.   1846.   *b* $1.
Rich's Dictionary of Roman and Greek Antiquities.   1873.
             b $1.
Richmond's Legal Form.   1854, no title.   *c* 50c.   1859.
                  b $1.   Supplement,   1860.   *b* 25c.
Ridley's View of the Civil and Ecclesiastical Law.   1662.
             b 50c.
Robbins' Ecclesiastical Statutes.   1791.   *h* $1.
Roberts on Fraudulent Conveyance.   1800.   *b* $1.   1800.
             c 75c.   1805.   *b* $1.25.
             on Statute of Frauds.   1805.   *b* $1.   1805.
             a $1.50.
             on Wills.   2 vols.   1826.   *b* $1.
             and Wallace Employers' Liability Act.   1881.
             2 copies.   *b* each 50c.
Robinson and Harrison's Digest.   U. C. Reports.   1852
             4 copies.   *b* each $3.

Robson on Bankruptcy. 1872. *b* $1.1873. *a* $1.50.
1876. *b* $2.

Rogers on Elections. 1880. 2 copies. *a* each $5. 1880.
b $4.50.

Judicature Acts. 1875. $1.

Law and Medical Men. 1884. *b* $1.25.

Roper on Husband and Wife. 2 vols. 1826. *b* $1.50.
on Legacies. 2 vols. 1804. *b* 50c. 1828. *c* $1.

Rordan's Conveyancer. Can., 1867. *b* 50c. 3rd edition.
b 50c.

Law List. 3 copies. 1882. *b* each 50c.

Roscoe's Criminal Evidence. Am., 1840. *b* 50c. 1854.
b $1. 1857. *b* $1. 1861. *b* $1. 1862. 2
copies. *b* each $1.25. 1866. *a* $2. 1866.
b $1.50. 1868. *c* $1.50.

Nisi Prius. Am., 1832. *b* 50c. 1858. *b* 75c.
1861. *b* $1. 1866. *c* $1.50. 1866. 6 copies.
b each $1. 1866.*a* $1.50. 1870. *b* $2.50.
1875. 2 copies. *b* each $5. 1879. *b* $6.

Ross on Vendors and Purchasers. 1826. 3 copies. *b*
each 50c.

Rules Sup. Court of Canada. 1876. 2 copies. *b* each 25c.

Russell on Awards. 1856. *b* $1. 1856. *c* 75c. 1870.
2 copies. *a* each $2.50.
on Factors and Brokers. 1844. *c* 50c.

Ryland's Crown Circuit Companion. 1836. *c* $1.

S

Sansum's Insurance Digest. 1876. Am., *b* $5.00.

Sandars on Uses and Trusts. 1791. *b* 25c. 1792.
1 vol. *b* 25c. 1813. 2 vols. *c* $1.00. 1844. *a*
$1.50.

Saunder's Pleadings and Evidence. 2 vols. Am., 1844.
b $3.00. 1851. From last English. 2 vols.
in 3. 4 copies. *b* each $12. 2 vols. 1851.
a $12.

Saunder's Municipal Registration and Elections.   1873.
    b 50c.

        Negligence.   1871.   *b* $1.
        Precedents of Indictments.   1872.   *b* $2.
        Warranties.   1874.   *b* $1.
Say's Political Econony.   Am., 1832.   *b* $1.
Scintillæ Jurist.   1879.   *b* 50c.
Scottish Anecdotes by Grant.   1885.   *b* 40c.
Scratchley on Bldg Soc.   1849.   *b* 50c.
Scriven on Copyhold.   2 vols.   1833.   2 copies.   *c* each
    $1.50.   1846.   *c* $4.
Schouler on Bailments.   Am., 1880.   *a* $3.
Sebastian on Trade Marks.   1878.   6 copies.   *b* each
        $2.50.

        Digest of Trade Marks.   1879.   *b* $4.50.
Sedgwick on Damages.   2 vols.   Am., 1868.   *b* $5.
        Constitutional Law.   Am., 1874.   2 copies.
        b each $5.00.
Selwyn's Nisi Prius.   2 vols.   1838.   *b* 50c.
Seton on Decrees.   1830.   2 copies.   *b* each 50c.   1854.
    a $1.
Sewell on Sheriff.   1842.   *b* 75c.
Shaen & Greville's Chancery Costs.   1870.   2 copies.   *b*
    each $1.50.

Shand's Practice of the Court of Sessions.   1848.   2 copies.
    2 vols.   *c* each $2.

Shearwood's Abridgment of Law of Real Property.   1876.
    b $1.50.

Sheldon on Subrogation.   Am., 1882.   *b* $3.
Shelford on Marriage and Divorce.   Am., 1841.   *b* $2.
        on Railways.   2 vols.   Am., 4 copies.   1855.   *b*
        each $3.
        Real Property Statutes.   1850.   2 copies.   *b* each
            $1.   1863.   *b* $2.   Last edition.   1874.
            b $2.25.
Shirley's Leading Cases.   1880.   2 copies.   *a* each $1.
    1883.   3 copies.   *a* each $2.   1883.   3 copies.   *b*
    each $1.50.

Sills' Bankruptcy. 1870. 18 copies. *b* each 50c.

Sinclair's Division Court Law. Can., 1879. *a* $5. 1879.
  b $4. 1880. *c* $2. 1884. 2 copies. *b* each $2.50.
  1885. *a* $3. 1885. *c* $2.50. 1886. *a* $1.50.

Sladden Registry Law. 1857. *c* 50c.

Sleigh's Hand Book Criminal Law. 1858. *b* 25c. 1864.
  4copies. *b* each 50c.

Sloan's Legal Register. Am., 1878. 2 copies. *b* each
  50c.

Smith's Action at Law. 1848. *b* 25c. 1857. *b* 25c.
  Chancery Practice. Am., 2 vols. 1837. *b* $2.
    1862. 2 copies. *b* each $4.
  Common Law. 1878. *c* $1.50. 1880. *a* $2.50.
  Contracts. Am., 1858. *c* 25c. 1858. *b* 50c.
    1856. 3 copies. *b* each 50c.
  Compendium for Lawyers and Business Men. Am.,
    1875. *b* $1.
  Equity Jurisprudence. 1878. *b* $1.50. 1880.
    a $2.50.
  Hand Book of Partnership. 1872. *b* 25c.
  Hand Book of Bills, Cheques and Notes. 1859.
    b 25c.
  Legal Forms. 1875. *b* 25c.
  Leading Cases. 2 vols. 2copies. 1837. *c* each
    $2.50. 2 vols. 1856. *b* $1. Am., 2 vols.
    1844. *b* $1. 1849. *b* $1.50. 1879. 2 vols.
    b $8. 1879. 2 copies. *a* each $9.
  Reinbursement of Property. 1855. *b* 25c. Am.,
    1856. *b* 50c.
  Mercantile Law. 1857. *b* $1. 1858. *b* $1.
    1864. 4 copies. *b* each $2. 1865. *b* $2.
    Am., 1872. *b* $3.50.
  Negligence. 1880. 2 copies. *a* each $2.25.
  Real and Personal Property. Am., 1865. *b* $1.50.
  Theory of Moral Sentiments, etc. 2 vols. in 1.
    Am., 1817. *b* $1.50.

Snell's Principles of Equity. 1868. 2 copies. *b* each $1.50.
    1872. *a* $2.50. Am., 1882. *c* $3. 1884. *a* $4.50.

Snelling and Jones' Chancery Orders. 1879. 4 copies.
  b each $1.

Somer's Scotch Banks and their Systems of Issue. 1873.
  b $1.

Spear's Extradition. 1879. *b* $3.

Spence's Equitable Jurisdiction. 2 vols. Am., 1846. *b* $4.

Speeches by Celebrated Irish Orators. *c* $1.

Stanhope's Rights of Juries. 1792 $1.50.

Starkie's Slander and Libel. 1830   vl. 1. *b* $1.
          on Evidence. 1853. 2 vols. 2 copies. *b* each
              25c. 1860. Am. *b* $1.

Steer's Parish Law. 1830. *c* 25c.

Stephen's Criminal Law. 1877. 4 copies. *b* each $2.50.
              1877. *a* $3. 1883. 2 copies. *a* each $3.25.
              1883. 4 copies. *b* each $3.

          Commentaries. 1874. 4 vols. *b* $12. Vols.
              2, 3 and 4. Am., 1843. *b* each 50c.

          Digest of Evidence. Am., 1877. *b* 75c. Am.,
              1879. *b* $1.

          Joint Stock Companies. Can., 1881. *a* $6.50.

          Nisi Prius. 3 vols. Am., 1844. 3 copies. *b*
              each $4.

          Pleadings. 1824. *c* 25c. 1838. *b* 25c. Am.,
              1841. *b* 50c. Am., 1845. *b* 50c. Am.,
              1851. *b* 75c. Am., 1859. *b* $1. 1860. *a* $1.50.
              1860. *c* $1.

          Questions on Commentaries. 1869. *b* $1.50.

Stevens' Average. 1818. *c* $1.50. 1822. *c* $1.50.
          Indictable Offences. Can., 1880. *a* $1.25.
          Rules of Court. Can., 1880. *b* 50c.

Stewart on Conveyancing. 3 vols. 1882. 2 copies. *b*
  each $2. 1846. 2 vols. *b* $3.

St. Leonard's Property Laws. 1858. *c* 25c. Am., 1858. 2
  copies. *b* each 25c.

Stone's on Building Societies. 1851. *b* 50c.
          Councillors Manual. 1872. 2 copies. *b* each 50c.
          Petty Sessions. 1863. *b* 50c.

Story on Agency. Am., 1839. 2 copies. *b* 75c. 1839. *c*
    each 50c. 1851. *b* $1. 1874. *a* $3.50.
  Bailments. Am., 1863. *b* $1.50.
  Conflict of Laws. 1841. *b* $1. 1841. *c* 50c.
    1846. *b* 50c. Am. 1852. *b* $1. Am., 1857.
    b $1.
  on the Constitution. 1851. 2 copies. *b* each $2.
    1858. *b* $3.
  Equity Jurisprudence. 2 vols. 1836. *b* $1. 1839.
    c $1.50. 1839. *b* $1. Am., 1846. *b* $2.
    1853. *b* $3. 1861. 7 copies. *b* each $4.
    1873. vol. 2. *a* $2. 1877. 2 copies. *a*
    each $7.
  Equity Pleadings. Am., 1848. *b* 50c. 1865. *b*
    $2. 1879. *b* $3.50.
  on Partnership. 1841. 3 copies. *b* each 50c. Am.
    1859. *b* $1.
  Pleadings in Civil Actions. 1329. *b* 50c.
  on Promissory Notes. 1848. 2 copies. *c* each 50c.
    1845. *b* $1. 1847. 2 copies. *b* each $1. 1860.
    b $2.
Story's Sales. Am., 1847. *b* $1. 1853. *b* $2.50.
Sugden on Powers. 1823. Am., *b* 50c. 1849. *b* $1.50.
  1856. Am., *b* $2.
    on Vendors and Purchasers. 1830. *c* 50c. 2
      vols. 1834. *b* 50c. 3 vols. 1839. *a* 50c.
      Am., 3 vols. in 2. 1843. *b* 50c. 2 vols.
      1846. *c* $1. 1851. *b* $2.
Surrogate Court Rules. Can., 1858. *b* 50c.
Swinburn on Wills. 1677. *b* 40c. 1793. *b* $1.
Sweet's Forms of Conveyancing. 1845. *b* $1.50.

T

Taschereau's Criminal Law. 2 vols. Can., 1870-5. *a* $3.
    Code of Civil Procedure. Can. 1876. 2
      copies. *b* each $5.

Taylor's Civil Law. 1828. *c* $1.50.

  Chancery Orders. Can. 1860. interleaved *b* $1.
   1860. 2 copies. *a* each 50c. 1863. *c* $1.
   1868. *c* $4. 1868. 10 copies. *b* each $5.
   1868. 4 copies interleaved. *b* each $5.50.

  on Evidence. 2 vols. 1848. *c* $1. 1855. 2
   copies. *c* each $2.50. 1858. *b* $2.50. 1864.
   2 copies. *b* each $4.50. 1864. 2 copies. *a*
   each $5. 1868. *b* $5. 1868. *c* $4. 1872.
   b $6. 1878. 3 copies. *b* each $8.

  Medical Jurisprudence. 1873. *b* $5. 1874. 2
   copies. *b* each.

  on Poisons. Am., 1848. *b* $1.

  on Titles. 1873. 2 copies. *b* each 75c.

  and Ewart's Practice. Can., 1881. *a* $3. 10
   copies. *b* each $2.50.

  Presbyterian Statutes. 1879. *b* 75c.

Theobald's Principal and Surety. 1882. 2 copies. *c*
  each $1.

  Wills. 1881. *c* $3.

Thomas' Universal Jurisprudence. 1828. *c* 25c.

Thompson's Law of the Farm. Am., 1876. *a* $3.

  Liability of Officers and Directors. Am., 1880.
   a $4.

  on Benefit Building Societies. 1850. *c* 50c.

Tidd's Forms. 1809. *b* 75c. 1819. *c* 50c. 1840.
  b $1.

  Practice. 2 vols. 1817. 2 copies. *b* each $1.
   1821. *c* $1. 1824. *b* $1.50. 1828. *a* $2.
   1837. *c* $2. 1837. *b* $2.50. Am., 1840.
   2 copies. scarce. *b* each $9 Supplements.
   1830. *b* $1. 1830. *c* 75c. 1833. *c* $1.

  Rules K. B. and C. P. 1832. *a* 75c. 1832.
   c 50c.

Tiffany's Registration. 1881. *a* $3.

Todd's Private Bill Practice. Can. 1862. *c* 25c. 1868.
  b 50c.

  Parliamentary Law. Can. 1840. 2 copies. *b* each
   $1.

Toller on Executors. 1818. *b* 25c. 1822. *c* $1.
Tomlin's Digested Index to the Term Reports. 1812. *b*
50c.
Toronto City Council Minutes. 1867-8 and 1869. *a* each
$1.
Tower on Juries. 1784. *b* 50c.
Travis on the Constitution of Canada. 1884. *c* $1.
Trayner's Latin Maxims. 1883. *a* $6.
Trevor's Taxes on Succession. 1856. *b* 25c.
Tremaine's Pleas of the Crown. 1793. *b* 50c.
Trials, City of Glasgow Bank. 1879. *c* 25c.
Tripp's Chancery Forms. 1858. *a* 50c.
       Charitable Trusts. 1862. *b* 50c.
Tudor's Leading Cases on Mercantile and Maritime Law.
       1868. 3 copies. *b* each $5. Am., 1873. 2
       vols. 2 copies. *b* each. $8.
       on Conveyancing. 1863. 2 copies. *b* each $2.50.
Turner on Contract of Pawn. 1863. *b* 50c.
       Costs in High Court Chancery. 1804. Vol 1. 50c.
       on Quieting Titles. Can., 1867. *c* 50c.
Tyrwhitt on Pleading. 1846. *b* 50c.
Tyler on Infancy and Coverture. Am., 1873. *b* $3.

U

Underhill on Trusts. 1878. *b* $1.50.
United States Crim. Digest. 1856. *b* 50c.
               Foreign Relations. 1877-8. 2 vols. *b* $1.

V

Vacher's Stamp Digest. 1871. *b* 25c.
Valpy's Schrevelius' Greek Lexicon. 1847. *b* $1.
Van Heythusen's Equity Draftsman. 2 vols. 1828. 2
       copies. *c* each. $2. 1861. *b* $5.
Vattel's Law of Nations. 1760. 2 vols. in 1. *b* $1.
Vaucher's Marine Ins. 1836. *b* $1.

W

Wallace's Reporters. Am., 1882. *a* $3.

Walkem's Married Women's Property Act. 1874. *b* $1.

        on Wills. Can., 1873. 4 copies. *b* each $4.

Walker on Executors. 1880. *a* $4.

Washburn's Easements and Servitudes. Am., 1867.
        b $2.

        Real Property. Am., 1868. Vols. 1 and 3.
        b $3.

Watkins on Conveyancing. Am., 1838. *b* $1. 1845. 4
        copies. *b* each $2. 1845. 2 copies. *c* each
        $1.50.

        on Copyholds. 2 vols. 1826. *b* $1.50. 1825.
        2 vols. 2 copies. *b* each $2.

        on Descents. 1801. *c* 25c.

Watson on Arbitrations. 1825. *c* 25c. 1846. *a* $1.

        Compendium of Equity. 1873. 2 vols. 3 copies.
        b each $2.

        on Partnership. 1807. 2 copies. *b* each 50c.
        1807. *c* 25c.

        Powers of Canadian Parliaments. 1880. 2 copies.
        b each 50c.

        on Sheriff. 1827. *c* 50c.

Weightman's Medical Practitioner's Legal Guide. 1870.
        a 50c.

Well's Questions of Law and Fact. Am., 1879. *a* $3.

Wentworth on Pleading. 10 vols. 179˙. *b* $6.

West on Extents. 1817. 2 copies. *c* each 50c.

Westlake's Private International Law. Am., 1859. *b* $1.50.

Wharton's Articled Clerk's Manual. 1854. *c* 50c. 1864.
        b $1.

        Conflict of Laws. Am., 1872. *a* $3.

        Conveyancer. Am., 1851. 3 copies. *b* 50c.

        Criminal Law. 2 vols. Am. 1880. *a* $10.

        Pleas of Indictments. 2 vols. 1871. *b* $7.

        Law Lexicon. 1864. *b* $1.50.

Wheaton's International Law. Am., 1855. *b* $2.

Wheelhouse's Corrupt Practice Prevention Act. 1883. *a* $1.

White and Tudor's Leading Cases in Equity. 2 vols. 1866. *a* $4. 1877. 2 copies. *a* each $7.

Whiteway's Hints. 1883. *b* $1.

Whitworth's Equity Precedents. 1848 *b* $1.

Wicksteed's Index Statutes of Canada. 1854. *b* $1.
> Index to Statutes of U. Can. 1856. *b* $1.

Wigram on Discovery. 1840. 3 copies. *c* each $1. 1840. *a* $1.25.
> on Extrinsic Evidence in Wills. 1834. *c* 50c.

Wilkinson on Replevin. 1825. *b* 50c.

Willard's Equity Jurisprudence. Am., 1875. *a* $3.

Williams on Seisin. 1878. *b* $1.
> Bankruptcy Practice. 1876. 3 copies. *a* each $2.
> on Executors. 2 vols. 1841. *b* $1. Am., 1841. *b* $1. Am., 1855. 2 vols. $1.50. 1856. $2. Am., 1859. 4 copies. *b* each $2.
> Personal Property. 1864. *c* $2.
> Questions on Real Property. 1866. *b* 50c.

Williams' Real Property. Am., 1857. *b* $1. 1859. *c* $1. 1862. *b* $1. 1865. *b* $1.50. 1872. *b* $1.75.
> and Bruce's Admiralty. 1869. *a* $4.

Willis on Trustees. 1827. 2 copies. *c* each 50c.

Wills on Circumstantial Evidence. Am., 1853. *b* $1.

Wilson's Ontario Municipal Acts. Can., 1870. 5 copies. *b* each 50c.
> Judicature Act. 1878. *a* $1.

Winslow's Lectures on Insanity. 1854. *b* $1.

Withy on Annuities. 1800. *b* 25c.

Wood's Conveyancing. 6 vols. 1792. *b* $3.
> Fire Insurance. Am., 1878. *b* $3.50.
> Master and Servant. Am., 1877. 2 copies. *a* each $4.
> Registry Act. 1866. *a* 25c.

Wolferstan on Election Petitions. 1869. *b* $1.

Woolsey's International Law. Am., 1870. 3 copies. *b*
        each $1.25.
Woolrych's Commercial and Mercantile Law. 1829. *c* 50c.
        Enclosure Act. 1846. *c* 50c.
        on Rights of Common. 1824. *c* 50c.
Wooddeson's Lectures on the Law of England. 1792. 2
        vols. *b* $1.
Woodfall's Landlord and Tenant. 1843. *b* 75c.
Wordsworth on Mining, Gas and other Companies. 1851.
        c 50c. 1854. *c* $1.
        Practice of Elections. 1832. *c* 50c.
Wotherspoon's Insolvent Act. Can., 1875. *a* 50c.
        Manual of Procedure. Can., 1870. *a* $1.50.
Wright's Advice on Study and Practice of the Law. 1824.
        c 75c.
Wrong's and Rights of a Traveller. Can., 1875. *b* $1.

Y

Young's Historical Sketch of the French Bar. 1869. *b* $1.

REPORTS.

Collect'ons of the various Courts offered at specially Low Prices to clear off our shelves.

[*Where no dates are given there is but one edition published.*]

ALL THE FOLLOWING VOLUMES ARE IN GOOD LIBRARY CONDITION ; MANY ARE IN NEW BINDING.

Chancery Reports. 1557 to 1866 ; nearly complete set.

Cary, 1665 ; Tothill, 1649 ; Dickens, 2 vols., 1803 ; Nelson, 1717 ; Equity Cases Abridged, 1732 ; Freeman, 1823 ; Vernon, 2 vols., 1829 ; Finch's Precedents, 1792 ; Peere Williams, 3 vols., 1793 ; Gilbert, 1740 ; Cases temp. Talbot, 1793 ; Atkyns, 3 vols., 1761 ; Ambler, 2 vols., 1828 ; Eden, 2 vols., 1818 ; Romilly's Notes ; Brown, by Belt, 4 vols., 1820 ; Cox, 2 vols., 1824 ; Vesey, Jr., and Hovenden's Suppt., 22 vols., 1827 ; Vesey and Beames, 3 vols., 1818 ; G. Cooper : Merivale, 3 vols. ; Swanston, 3 vols. ; Jacob and Walker, 2 vols. ; Jacob : Turner and Russell ; Russell, 5 vols. ; Russell and Mylne, 2 vols. ; Mylne and Keen, 3 vols. ; Mylne and Craig, 5 vols. ; Craig and Phillips : Phillips, 2 vols. ; Macnaghten and Gordon, 3 vols ; DeGex, McN. and Gordon, 8 vols ; DeG. and Jones, 4 vols ; DeG., Fisher and Jones, 4 vols. ; DeG., Jones and Smith, 4 vols. All in good condition ; some few are American editions, but full reprints. 106 volumes for $240.

Roll's Court, 1829-1826.

Tamlyn ; Keen, 2 vols. ; Beaven, 36 vols. Good second hand 39 vols. for $235.

English Chancery Reports.

American Reprints containing the following reports :
V. C. Ct., Simons and Stuart, 2 vols. ; Simons, 17 vols.;
Simons, N. S., 2 vols. ; Hare, 11 vols. ; Collyer, 2 vols. ;
Young and Collyer, 2 vols. ; Tamlyn ; Keen, 2 vols. ;
Russell, 5 vols. ; Russell and Mylne, 2 vols. ; Mylne
and Keen, 3 vols. ; Mylne and Craig, 5 vols. ; Craig
and Phillips ; G. Cooper ; Phillips, 2 vols. ; MacNachten and Gordon, 3 vols ; DeGex, MacNachten and Gordon, 8 vols. ; DeGex and Jones, 4 vols. ; DeGex, Fisher
and Jones, 4 vols. ; DeGex, Jones and Smith, 4 vols.
In all, 81 volumes, for $195.

King's and Queen's Bench Reports.   A nearly complete set
from 1066 to 1866, all in good library condition,
many of which are scarce.

Placita Anglo-Normannicum, 1879 ; Keilway, 1633 ;
Moore, 1663 ; Leonard, 1658 ; Plowden, 2 vols., 1792;
Owen, 1656 ; Noy, 1656; Coke, 6 vols., 1826 ; Croke,
4 vols., 1790 ; Goldsboro, 1653 . Popham, 1656 ; Yel-
verton, 1792 ; Hobart, 1650 ; Calthrop, 1872; Bul-
strode, 1657 ; Rolle, 2 vols., 1675 ; Palmer, 1678 ; W.
Jones. 1675 ; Latch, 1662 ; Aleyn, 1681 ; Siderfin,
1683 ; T. Raymond, 1803 ; Levinz, 3 vols. in 2, 1702 ;
Keble, 3 vols., 1685 ; Saunders, 3 vols., 1845 ; T. Jones,
1695 ; Ventris, 1716 ; Modern, 12 vols., 1793-96 ;
Freeman, 1826 ; Shower, by Butt, 1836 ; Comberback,
1724 ; Carthew, 1728 ; Salkeld, 1773 ; Lord Raymond,
3 vols., 1792 ; Comyns, 2 vols, 1792 ; Session's Cases,
1750; Strange, 2 vols., 1795 ; Fitzgibbon, 1732 ;
Barnes' Practice Cases, 2 vols., 1754 ; Andrews, 1791 ;
W. Blackstone, 2 vols., 1828 ; Kenyon, 2 vols. ; Bur-
rows, 5 vols, 1812; Lofft, 1790; Cowper, 2 vols.,
1800 ; Douglas, 4 vols., 1790 ; Durnford and East, 8
vols., 1788 ; East, 16 vols. ; Maule and Selwyn, 6
vols. ; Barnewall and Alderson, 5 vols. ; Barn. and
Cresswell, 10 vols. ; Barn. and Adolphus, 5 vols. ; Adol.
and Ellis, 12 vols ; Q. B., 18 vols.; Ellis and Blackburn,
8 vols. ; Ellis, Bl. and El. ; Ellis and Ellis, 3 vols. ;

King's and Queen's Bench Reports—*Continued.*

Best and Smith, 6 vols. Some few are American editions but are full reprints. 186 volumes $325.

Bail Court. 1819-1852.

Chitty, 2 vols. ; Dowling, 9 vols. ; Dowling, N. S., 2 vols.; Dowling and Lowndes, 7 vols. ; Lowndes, Maxwell and Pollock, 2 vols. ; Lowndes and Maxwell. 23 vols., $40.

Revised Statutes of United States. 1873-1845 in 1 volume, and 2 supplements being vols. 22 and 23 ; in all, 3 vols. ; good second hand $9.

Upper Canada Reports. 1823 to 1887.

Taylor's K. B., 1 vol; Draper's K. B., 1 vol. ; Q. B. O. S., 6 vols. ; Queen's Bench, 45 vols. ; Common Pleas, 32 vols. ; Chancery (Grants), 29 vols. ; Practice, 11 vols. ; Error and Appeal, 3 vols. ; Com. L. Chambers, 2 vols.; Chancery Chambers, 4 vols.; Ont. Appeal, 13 vols.; Ontario Reports, 13 vols. 161 vols., new half calf, $805. Four sets of above 161 vols. in good second hand condition, each $644.

Upper Canada Reports. 1823-1867.

Taylor's K. B., 1 vol. ; Draper's K. B., 1 vol.; K. B. O. S., 6 vols.; Queen's Bench, 25 vols.; Common Pleas, 16 vols. ; Chancery, 12 vols. ; Chancery Chambers, vol. 1 ; Practice, vols. 1-2, 3 ; Error and Appeal, 3 vols; Com. Law Chambers, 2 vols. 70 vols. new half calf, $310. Special price for time payments.

Upper Canada Reports. 1867-1887.

Queen's Bench, 26 to 46, 21 vols. ; Common Pleas, 17 to 32, 16 vols. ; Chancery, 13 to 29, 17 vols. ; Chancery Chambers, 2, 3, 4, 3 vols. ; Practice, 4 to 11, 8 vols. ; Ontario Appeal, 1 to 13, 13 vols. ; Ontario Reports, 1 to 13, 13 vols. 91 vols., new half calf, $455. We have in stock a large number of odd volumes of the above, both new and second hand, which can be had at moderate figures.

Lower Canada Reports.

Perrault, 2 vols.; Pyke; Stuart's K. B.; Revue de Legislation, 3 vols.; L. C. Reports, 17 vols.; Seignorial Questions, 2 vols.; Jurist, 31 vols.; Law Journal, 4 vols.; Revue Legale, 15 vols.; Revue Critique, 3 vols.; Quebec Law Reports, 13 vols.; Legal News, 10 vols.; La Themis, 5 vols.; Dorion. 4 vols.; Montreal Law Reports, 6 vols.; Stephen's Digest, 3 vols.; Stuart's Vice-Admiralty, 2 vols. All in good binding, mostly new; 122 volumes for $675.

Howell's State Trials and Index, 34 vols. Fine copy for $110.

Common Pleas. 1486 to 1866.

Benloe and Dalison, 1689; Anderson, 1664; Brownlow and Goldesborough, 1654; Saville, 1675; Hutton, 1656; Winch, 1657; Littleton, 1683; Hetley, 1657; Carter, 1688; Vaughan, 1677; Wilson, 3 vols., 1799; Willes, 1800; H. Blackstone, 2 vols., 1827; Bosanquet and Puller, 5 vols., 1826; Taunton, 8 vols.; Broderip and Bingham, 3 vols.; Bingham, 10 vols.; Bingham's N. C., 6 vols.; Manning and Granger, 7 vols.; Common Bench, Am., 18 vols.; Common Bench, N. S., Am., 19 vols. All in good condition; 92 vols. $200.

Harrison and Rutherford; Marshal, 2 vols.; Moore, 12 vols.; Moore and Payne, 5 vols.; Scott, 8 vols.; Scott, N. S., 8 vols. 36 vols. for $50.

English Common Law Reports.

118 vols. and Index, 3 vols. Containing Q. B. 1818-1865; C. B. 1813-1865; Nisi Prius, 1815-1849. Good second hand set; 158 vols. in 118, full reprints, $250. Another set, second hand, 40 vols. condensed, fair condition, $180. Another set, new, $300.

The above reports sold originally at $512; these, with the Exchequer Reports below, give a consecutive series of English Common Law cases from about 1813 to 1865, continued by " The Law Reports " from 1865 to 1887.

www.ingramcontent.com/pod-product-compliance
Lightning Source LLC
Chambersburg PA
CBHW021634270326
41931CB00008B/1012